GET HIGH

How to coach yourself for high
performance in your work

Dear Reader,

Wishing you the
best of high
performance!

Sangeeta

SANGEETA
SHANKARAN
SUMESH

INDIA • SINGAPORE • MALAYSIA

Notion Press

No.8, 3rd Cross Street
CIT Colony, Mylapore
Chennai, Tamil Nadu – 600004

First Published by Notion Press 2020
Copyright © Sangeeta Shankaran Sumesh 2020
All Rights Reserved.

ISBN 978-1-64899-972-7

This book has been published with all efforts taken to make the material error-free after the consent of the author. However, the author and the publisher do not assume and hereby disclaim any liability to any party for any loss, damage, or disruption caused by errors or omissions, whether such errors or omissions result from negligence, accident, or any other cause.

While every effort has been made to avoid any mistake or omission, this publication is being sold on the condition and understanding that neither the author nor the publishers or printers would be liable in any manner to any person by reason of any mistake or omission in this publication or for any action taken or omitted to be taken or advice rendered or accepted on the basis of this work. For any defect in printing or binding the publishers will be liable only to replace the defective copy by another copy of this work then available.

*Dedicating this book to
my father on his tenth anniversary*

THE TALK ABOUT THE BOOK

If you want to up your game, get to the next performance level and improve yourself, you need to read this book! Packed with real, actionable points in every chapter, Sangeeta will teach you how to achieve maximum potential in your professional life.

— Dr Marshall Goldsmith,
New York Times, bestselling author
& Thinkers 50 #1 Executive Coach

"Looking for the low-down on how to coach yourself to become the highest version of yourself? Look no further. Sangeeta shares practical, actionable advice to help you get better. Get this book. And then get ready to Get High."

— Prakash Iyer
Leadership Coach,
Motivational Speaker & Author

REVIEWS

'I strongly recommend Get High as an ideal D-I-Y guide to professional self-actualisation regardless of your age or position. Sangeeta is pithy, precise, punchy and extremely practical - All In One!'

— Sunil Subramaniam, Managing Director,
Sundaram Asset Management Company

"Sangeeta has created an excellent daily work management workbook for anyone to follow and plot your own way to High performance"

— VS Parthasarathy, President Mobility Services Sector,
Mahindra & Mahindra

Sangeeta has powered this book with tools for self-reflection, getting clarity for your goals, gaining insights for high performance and making it all happen. It simply helps you lead yourself in the challenging times of the new normal. I would say 'GET HIGH' is a must read.

— Shobhana Ravi, Chief IT, Innovation & Learning Officer, TAFE

"Achieving high performance by uplifting yourself and your service to others is the timely message of this vital book. Discover precious ideas and actions through this book to navigate well in the joy of living and giving."

— Ron Kaufman, New York Times Bestselling Author

CONTENTS

~

What the Author has to Say   *9*

Gratitude   *13*

Chapter 1   **Understanding High Performance**   **15**

Chapter 2   **Getting started**   **25**

Chapter 3   **The Driving Force**   **32**

Chapter 4   **Know Your Priorities**   **39**

Chapter 5   **Turn Off the Unwanted**   **46**

Chapter 6   **Track What's Important**   **54**

Chapter 7   **Step Out to Step Up**   **60**

Chapter 8   **Art of Self-Management**   **67**

Chapter 9   **Overcoming Fears**   **74**

Chapter 10   **Master What You Like**   **81**

Chapter 11   **Get Real**   **88**

Chapter 12   **What Next?**   **95**

Reflections on My High Performance Journey –
What I Have Achieved   *107*

Reflections on My High Performance Journey –
What I Learnt about Myself   *108*

What the Author has to Say

Why "Get High"?

How do you feel when you

- Accomplish a task with speed, efficiency and finesse?
- Achieve something that you thought you could not?
- Keep getting consistently better in what you do?

You will feel proud, happy and experience a sense of accomplishment, right? You get a kick and feel high and mighty about yourself, don't you? So when you achieve what you want to, you surely "Get High" about your own self!

That is what this book is about. **To enable you to get to a higher version of yourself so that you can achieve high performance in whatever you do.**

You may ask, *why high performance*? Well, who doesn't want high performance?! Be it individuals or organisations, everyone wants to be a high performer in their domain. And the truth is, everyone is a high performer. All that you need to do is channelise your performance in the right direction for exceptional results. In my journey as a High Performance (HiPer) Business coach, I realised that individuals can easily peak their potential by adopting a few strategies and be high performers in their domain. And it is these high performers who can make an organisation a high-performing one. Hence, businesses are always on the lookout for high performers and want the high-potential individuals to scale up to the next level of their performance.

While many want high performance, I realised, during my coaching conversations with my clients, that a few common challenges come in the way of high performance, thus making them feel stuck and unable to progress. I worked with them and helped them overcome these challenges. When I looked back, I noticed that some of these challenges were common across people, irrespective of their personal or professional goals or the nature and size of business.

Hence, I am sharing with you a few of the anecdotes in this book, which will aid your growth and high performance. As all coaching conversations are confidential, the names mentioned in the chapters have been changed.

WHY THIS BOOK NOW?

I am writing this book during the business lockdown period due to the Corona pandemic. During this time, many known people reached out to me for various things, and one thread they all seemed to have in common was to get better and grow for the days after the pandemic. What pulled their morale down was the negativity, fear and uncertainty looming over. To make them feel better, as a HiPer coach, I want to induce positivity in the current atmosphere and do my bit to inspire and motivate people as much as possible.

Thus was born the idea of this book, wherein I thought I would share my knowledge on ways to overcome challenges and be on the path of high performance. In the current scenario, I thought this would be apt so that the days ahead can be brighter, both personally and professionally, for everyone.

Remember – To move up the performance level, to get a sense of accomplishment, to feel better about yourself and to be the high performer that you want to be, you just require one thing—**your desire.** Your desire to improve, your desire to get better, your desire to overcome your challenges, your desire to find clarity, your desire to find solutions and so on.

With this keen intent, are you ready to get started on your high-performance journey?

How is this book different?

As "The Gain Enabler", I want you to gain out of the various experiences and learnings of others. That apart, I have shared easy tools and activities so that you can coach yourself to get to the next level.

This book is a quick read with byte-sized, easily-actionable points at the end of each chapter. It is clubbed with food for thought, which will enable you to be on the path of high performance both in your personal and professional life. It further contains keys to unlock and maximise your growth.

How will this book help you?

While it is extremely beneficial to have an external coach, in this book, I am going to take you through how you can coach yourself to achieve high performance.

If you are someone wanting to up your game, get to the next level of performance and become an improved and better version of yourself, then this book is for you.

I have shared simple activities at the end of each chapter. If you think it will make it easier for you to accomplish your high-performance goals, I would recommend you to complete them. Alternatively, you also have a choice to complete the activities that are most meaningful for you and reflect on the questions at the end of each chapter.

Ready? Let's take off!

GRATITUDE

As a professional speaker, I have addressed many forums and gatherings on various aspects of high performance. The encouragement I received from the audience is where the trigger to write this book came from. Hence, I would first like to thank all the audience for inspiring me to write on high performance.

Next, I would want to thank my clients from the bottom of my heart, as they have indirectly contributed with their real-life stories, which has helped in shaping this book as well as making it an interesting read.

Grateful to Dr. Marshall Goldsmith & Prakash Iyer for their endorsement and words of praise for the book.

My family for always standing by me. Heartfelt thanks to my mother Sukanya Shankar, my husband Sumesh, my son Shrey and my daughter Svara for being there for me. I'm forever grateful for having them in my life.

Thankful to my beta readers, my husband Sumesh, my cousin Shweta Ganesh and friends Naveen Valsakumar, Pravin Shekar and Aswin Vaidyanathan, who helped in fine-tuning this book.

Special thanks to my daughter Svara for the artwork in the book and photographer Swasti Jain for my picture on the cover.

Last but not least, the wonderful team from Notion Press who helped with the editing, cover design and in contributing to the success of this book.

Chapter 1

Understanding
High Performance

"Achieving your extraordinary targets is high performance."

She was born in Hyderabad to national-level volleyball players. Her elder sister was a national-level handball player. Although her family was into sports, she initially wanted to pursue medicine. However, she was inspired by watching the success of a player in the game of badminton and, later, went on to become the first Indian woman to win an Olympic Silver medal. The lady was none other than P. V. Sindhu, who was awestruck seeing her coach's performance that she chose to play badminton. Sindhu's coach, as we know, is Pullela Gopichand. Sindhu was coached by him for many years and continues to train with him.

Now you are probably wondering whether you need to aspire to get an Olympic medal to be a high performer. Maybe you also assumed that Gopichand was her coach because he was an exceptional badminton player himself. What if I were to break this myth?

Listen to this second anecdote, which is about Ananth. Ananth was an engineer by profession and was passionate about music. He was not only a talented singer but also had the unique ability to create percussion sounds from within. However, despite having this unique talent, he lacked motivation, kept procrastinating and was not taking any steps to showcase his talents. Although he had a percussion teacher, he was irregular to his classes, was making excuses for himself and not making the time to practice and rehearse. He felt very disturbed that he was not able to do much despite having this special talent. The main challenge he felt was that he was unable to do much, as deep down, he had a fear of failure. He thought he was not good enough and had low levels of self-confidence, which came in his way of progress. Every time he wanted to break free from these thoughts, he was getting more caught up in them and was not progressing.

It was then that he chanced upon a high-performance coach and decided to seek help to better his situation. And do you know what happened? You thought he became an overnight success, right?! No, not at all. While there are situations where you could get an immediate solution by getting coached, there are situations that could take longer. The pace of progress depends on the circumstances, challenges and capabilities of each individual. So after about eight months of getting coached, Ananth transformed for the better. He ensured he attended his classes regularly, had the time to practice his lessons and became a much happier and self-confident person, pursuing his love of music along with his unique ability to perform acapella. He even went on to perform at local concerts, winning the hearts of many. Ananth has now moved notches up on his scale by his improved level of performance and is a much happier individual.

So like you notice, it is not necessary to win medals to be a high performer. When you achieve your own set targets of growth, you are a high performer.

Was Ananth's coach a musician? No, not at all. So it is true that the coach need not be a domain expert. That is probably making you wonder who a high-performance coach is and what a coach does.

A coach is not a teacher, not a mentor, not a counsellor, not a consultant and not necessarily a domain expert. A coach is one who partners with you, provokes your thoughts, inspires you to take action, allows you to reflect and helps you to get solutions to your challenges. A coach does not provide advice but facilitates your development and enhances your awareness.

While in sports, the positive impact a good coach has on the success of an individual or team is taken for granted—because they enhance skills through structured plans and set focussed goals—the fact is, the same applies to the executive world as well.

While you can work with an external coach, which has its own merits, I am also going to give you ways to coach yourself to achieve high performance. So you have a choice to work either with an external coach like me or choose to be your own coach. I have stated in each chapter, how you can self-coach and be on the path of high performance.

Let's start with the brass tacks of high performance.

WHAT IS HIGH PERFORMANCE?

Achieving superior results by performing at a high standard as per set targets is high performance. To state it simply, creating a newer, improved version of yourself. What is required for high performance? **Your desire to strive for the better and the keenness of your intent**

are important. In other words, exceeding your own expectations is high performance.

In the example above, Ananth had a keen desire to pursue his talent, and the superior results he obtained were by performing at a high standard. His performance level was getting better; he was showcasing his talent to a large audience and feeling very good within. The target he had set for himself was to perform in front of a large audience and be acknowledged and appreciated for this talent.

So to achieve high performance, you do not need to compete with others, but you compete with your own self to get better and achieve improved results. Comparing yourself to others and competing against other people will drain your energy. By competing with yourself, you only get better. If required, you can seek inspiration from role models and strive to get better at what you are doing.

Why high performance?

Whenever you want to progress in your life or achieve better results for yourself or move ahead in your life, high performance gets you there. You are benchmarking the yesterday's you with today's you, to get better.

From a feeling of being stuck and helpless, Ananth started progressing on his journey of high performance with his set specific goals by improving on his talent. He defined the superior results he wanted to achieve and thus started his high-performance journey.

Who is a high performer?

An individual or an organisation that achieves results efficiently and consistently, thereby improving performance levels.

Ananth improved his performance notches up with consistent practice. This got him special recognition from renowned musicians, which made him feel on top of the world.

WHERE DO YOU WANT HIGH PERFORMANCE?

An area of your choice, an area where you want to improve your performance, an area that interests you or whatever you choose. High performance can be in any walk of life.

It was clear to Ananth that he wanted to focus on his special talent and give a stellar performance to an audience and then work his way from there.

WHEN DO YOU WANT HIGH PERFORMANCE?

When you want to pull yourself up, feel good about your achievements, feel satisfied and get a sense of accomplishment, be on top of the charts or be a leader in your domain.

Ananth also realised that by doing so, he would get fame and carve a niche for himself in the music arena. He could even get some monetary benefits if he performed at concerts.

HOW TO ACHIEVE HIGH PERFORMANCE?

This is what this book is about. It will reveal ways you can channelise your high performance. You can learn from the stories in it, and it will also give you easily implementable hacks at the end of each chapter, which will help you to coach yourself.

Like how Ananth sought the help of an external coach, you have a choice to either get yourself a coach you can work with, or you can self-coach. If you think you can coach yourself, then read on to know how.

ACTIVITY

This activity is aimed at helping you to think, identify and explore the various aspects of your life that interest you and to help you grow in those areas to get to your high-performance level. Thereafter, make a mind map of it like in the sample below. After stating each of these areas in the mind map, explore possibilities of revenue generation from any of these to make it your full-time/part-time profession or another revenue stream for yourself. Of course, this is only optional. You can also state other areas, which do not generate revenue but give you a high sense of satisfaction.

What is the key to selecting these areas? Here is a test that it should pass. An easy acronym for you to remember.

How does the selected area/s make you feel?

H – Happy (When you enjoy doing what you are doing)

I – Inspired (When you want to do more)

G – Gainful (When you are benefitted – financially or otherwise)

H – Heroic (When you get a sense of achievement)

STEPS

1. Once the areas selected pass the above test, make a list of the various areas that interest you (for example, it can be related to your domain, your work, reading, writing, travelling, practising yoga, watching movies, hearing music, playing a sport, etc.)

2. Write a minimum of two (maximum six) such areas as per your interest.

3. Deep dive into each of the areas to see what you like about each of them, what you are good at.

4. What would you like to improve in each of them?

5. Prepare your map like in the sample given on the next page. Feel free to customise it as per your requirements.

6. Congrats! You have now identified the areas you need to work on for your high performance.

SAMPLE MIND MAP

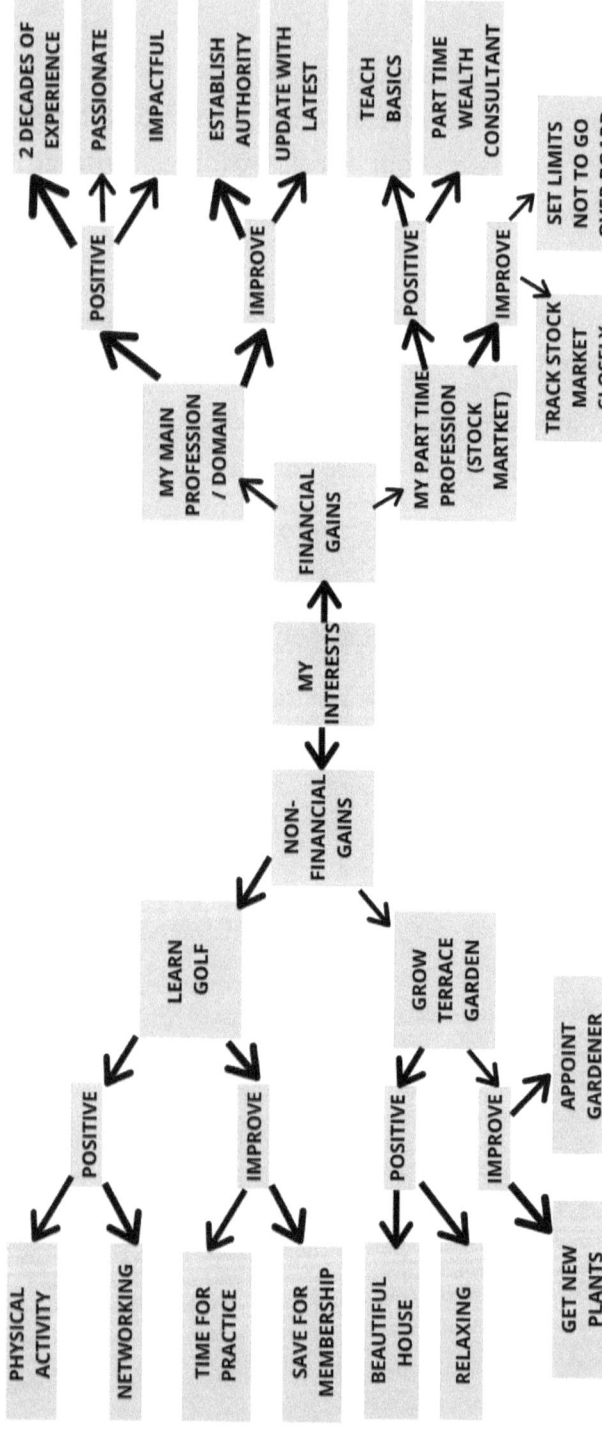

FILL IN YOUR MIND MAP BELOW

REFLECTION

- *What superior results would you like to accomplish?*

- *How do you intend to perform at high standards?*

- *What are the targets you want to set for yourself?*

SUMMARY

- *What, Why, Who, When, Where of high performance*

- *Who is a coach?*

- *Key to selecting your high performance areas*

Chapter 2

GETTING STARTED

"Defining your goals is the first step of high performance."

Puneet was identified as one of the high performers in a global multinational company. He was in his early thirties and was the youngest vice president in the organisation. His career growth was phenomenal, and his performance was exceptional. The organisation realised that Puneet had the potential to grow even further and hence assigned him a high-performance coach.

Puneet confessed to the coach that although his growth happened really fast, he was currently feeling stuck and uncertain about his future. This was because of a merger with another multinational as per the decision taken at the global headquarters. Puneet felt anxious about his career with these upcoming changes. His mind was clouded with many thoughts like who could be his next potential boss, what could be his next possible role, where would be his next work location, whether he should look out for other opportunities outside, etc. Due to this, his performance was not at its best.

During the coaching conversation, it appeared that Puneet had managed to be extremely successful in the past but was not able to do so in the current scenario. When asked what the differentiating factors under his control between his past and present were, Puneet realised something important.

He noticed a trend from the past. Each of his promotions was based on the goals he had set for himself. He wouldn't take any promotion that came his way. He would take it only if it took him closer to his goal of being the Asia Pacific Leader of his vertical. All his actions, like networking with the right people, selecting the right mentors within the organisation and building rapport with the teams based in other countries were carefully planned.

However, with the current changes, he had actually buried his career goal, as all he thought of was about the uncertainties and forgot about his aspirational goal. He realised he missed evaluating his decisions and the related actions that he needed to take, that would take him to his set goal. Puneet immediately started taking the necessary steps required.

WHAT CAN YOU LEARN FROM PUNEET'S STORY?

➢ *Most people go through phases of anxiety. Acknowledge it and see what needs to be addressed.*

➢ *You can only control the factors that are within your ambit.*

➢ *Know why you are doing what you are doing. Check if your actions are aligned to your goals.*

What is the case with you? What do you want to achieve? What do you aspire to be? What do you want? Further, remember, as mentioned in the book *"What got you here won't get you there"* by Dr. Marshall Goldsmith, you need to be looking at continuous improvements. So it is not that you achieve what you want and stop thereafter. Keep evolving to the next better version. So where do you start?

THE FIRST KEY IS TO HAVE A GOAL

Without setting yourself a goal, you will be like a headless chicken and lack direction. Therefore, set your high-performance goals.

To help you with it, here is an activity I would recommend you to complete. I urge you to complete the easy goal matrix listed below so that you know what you want to achieve by the time you finish reading this book.

This is a simple matrix to fill. This will serve as a reminder and will help you think, focus and develop on specific areas of your choice. This is also a good hack for you not to hide under the pretext of *"Oh, I forgot about it"* syndrome. Because once you fill it, you can put it up prominently so that it will serve you as a reminder to act on.

Here's what you have to do:

1. Select the top 3 areas you want to work on. If you want to focus only on one key area, start with just one. The choice is yours.

2. Rank the areas in the order of importance.

3. State 3 actions you want to perform under each of them that will take you closer to your objective. If you think there are only one or two actions that you need to complete, leave the other box(/es) empty.

4. Below are two sample matrices. You can customise the matrix as per your needs.

5. You can use this matrix format either for your individual goal or your business goals.

6. Other possible areas that you may want to work on can be financial, health, relationships, etc. Once you master them, you can go for other areas or on to higher levels in the same area.

SAMPLE PERSONAL GOAL MATRIX

Areas for high performance	Goals to be achieved by (date)	Measure / end goal	Action 1	Action 2	Action 3
Personal	*Reduce weight*	*10 kgs*	Mindful eating.	30 minutes workout, 4 times a week.	Sleep at least 7 hours each night.
Professional	*Upgrade skills in a particular domain*	*Secure a promotion during this appraisal*	Read one new book each month in the domain.	Learn from online courses.	Network with the domain experts for discussions.
Spiritual	*Better control of emotions*	*Feel inner peace (Score 7/10 on a scale of 10).*	Meditate for at least 15 minutes every day.	Say a gratitude prayer each day.	Practice breathing exercises every day.

SAMPLE BUSINESS GOAL MATRIX

Areas for high performance	Goals to be achieved by (date)	Measure / end goal	Action 1	Action 2	Action 3
Finance	*Increase profit.*	*Profit before tax margin to increase by 2%.*	Increase customer base by 10% through digital marketing.	Adopt zero-based budgeting.	Reduce interest costs by becoming debt-free.
Product	*Launch a high-end model with user-friendly features.*	*Dominate the market share by 60% with the new model.*	Upgrade technological know-how by investing in Research & Development.	Improve aesthetic design through the design experts.	Test new model for bugs and obtain feedback from users.
People	*Groom all department managers to be high performers.*	*Managers to achieve 90% of their targets.*	Replace the non-performing managers.	Set performance targets for each manager.	Assign external high-performance coach for each manager.

ACTIVITY

Complete your goal matrix.

Areas for high performance	Goals to be achieved by...	Measure/end goal	Action 1	Action 2	Action 3

REFLECTION

- *What do you want to achieve by the end of the specified goals?*

- *What happens if you do not achieve it within the set date? Are there any alternatives?*

- *How does the set goal help you in your growth?*

SUMMARY

- *It is essential to set goals.*

- *Identify your areas for high performance.*

- *Prepare your goal matrix.*

Chapter 3

THE DRIVING FORCE

"Be limitless. Be purposeful.
Be the high performer you want to be."

Krish had had an illustrious corporate career of 30 years. Thereafter, he had chosen to be an entrepreneur. But the business was not very lucrative. After about 4 years of the business venture, he decided to upskill himself and enrolled in an executive education MBA programme from a top-notch global business school. Upon completion of the course, Krish was elated to be an alumnus of the renowned business school.

Krish felt he had the relevant experience, and now qualification too, to become a CEO. This was his goal. He wanted to retire as the CEO of a large company. He was already 54 years old, and he wanted to serve as the CEO for the next few years before he could retire.

Despite being a subject matter expert with relevant experience and qualification, he was not considered CEO material by his prospective employers. He felt dejected as he was only used to success in interviews until then. Soon, this anxiety caused by an unsuccessful series of interviews started becoming a frustration for Krish. He kept wondering why he was not able to be successful. He wondered what he lacked while presenting himself to his prospective employers.

He brought this up for discussion with his coach. As the coaching conversation progressed, his coach probed on what his driving factor was to become a CEO, despite having been in senior leadership positions in his previous corporate roles. While his initial response was that it was for his talent, status, ego boost and the like, what actually emerged was something that was in his subconscious mind.

Krish gained the insight that he was, in fact, content with his career and, deep down, was not driven to become a CEO. He had succumbed to the pressure from his wife, who compared him with others. At every opportunity, she would take a dig at him for not being a CEO and not earning as much as others. This made him feel hurt. He felt if he became a CEO, she would be happy. However, the reality was he was not actually keen on being a CEO.

Once he realised that it was not his purpose but was only driven by his wife, he felt a lot lighter and at peace with himself. He felt what he actually wanted to do was grow his business and scale it. He decided he would focus his energy on his business rather than on becoming a CEO.

WHAT CAN YOU LEARN FROM KRISH'S STORY?

➢ *Know what you want. Keep checking this with yourself periodically.*

➢ *Upskill yourself in your relevant domains.*

➢ *Decide where you want to focus your energies.*

If you seek high performance, know your purpose and act on it. Anchor on your driving force for high performance.

Once your goal is set, deep dive to see why you have set these goals for yourself. A common issue that I noticed is a lack of clarity or not knowing why you want to achieve the goals or why you want to excel in the chosen area. What is your driving factor in getting to the next level? What do you truly want to achieve for yourself?

"Purposefulness" is the key,
which will help you achieve your goals

Know the purpose behind your desired actions. Knowing your purpose makes you feel more determined and, thereby, propels you forward. It aids you in the manifestation of your goal and leads you towards high performance. Get to know why you are doing what you are doing. First, get clarity in your head. And if you are satisfied with your answer, go for it.

Once you are clear about your purpose, here are the next steps that you can take:

1. List the benefits of accomplishing your goal.

2. State the result or the measure of success (as the case may be) of what you want to achieve.

3. Visualise how you would feel when you achieve your set target.

4. Next, list the factors that come in the way of accomplishing the goals so that you know what you have to overcome.

5. Think of ways to tackle the above factors.

6. Lastly, write down how you intend to keep a tab on your progress.

In a business context, there are times when the business owners or the leadership team fails to communicate the intentions behind certain goals or the purpose behind the action stated to the team. By clarifying the need for the specified action and telling them the purpose behind the expected outcome, individuals are motivated to perform better and contribute better. Even if it is obvious, state it, so that it is re-emphasised.

Another thing I want to draw your attention to is that it is not necessary to be a high performer in all areas. Instead, achieve mastery in one area after another that is related to your purpose and helps with your objectives. This is called **purposeful high performance**.

If you would like to add more fizz to the process, you can gamify it. Breakdown the steps required for your desired outcome. Set each step as the goal you want to achieve. For every goal you achieve, award yourself marks. (Alternatively, you also use online apps like Talking Timer, Habitshare and QTally to time your activity, stick to your habits or gamify as the case may be). Once you reach a certain number of points, reward yourself. Just remember that you are the referee and you are the player as well.

Complete the activity below, and in the next chapter, I shall reveal how to get another notch closer towards your high-performance target.

ACTIVITY

Purposefulness for my goal

State Goal:

The purpose of achieving my goal:

1. _____

_____

_____

2. _____

_____

_____

3. _____

_____

_____

My purposefulness steps:

1. _____

_____

_____

2. _____

_____

_____

3. _____

_____

_____

GAMIFICATION SCORECARD TEMPLATE

Task No.	Task Details	Date	Points	Cumulative Points	Reward Redemption
1					
2					
3					
4					
5					

REFLECTION

- *How will you know that your purpose and your goal are in alignment with each other?*

- *How does the purpose make you feel when you think about your goal?*

- *What could be some other hidden purposes behind the stated goals?*

SUMMARY

- *Know your purpose.*

- *List your purposefulness steps.*

- *Achieve purposeful high performance.*

- *Gamify the process.*

Chapter 4

KNOW YOUR PRIORITIES

"Increased awareness of
priorities leads you to high performance."

Tejas had grand plans for scaling and growing his business. He was very excited about presenting his business plans to his coach. After hearing him out, what the coach did was to challenge his ambitious plans. During the coaching conversation, it occurred to Tejas that while the plan looked good on paper, he was not being realistic. His ambition seemed to have blurred his vision from reality. He realised that his plans seemed theoretical and not practical. The growth priorities were skewed. Thus, his awareness grew that, in reality, he would never be able to achieve the projected numbers. This was his hard-hitting takeaway, but at the same time, it dawned on him that he needed to rephrase his business strategy. The first session of coaching shook him up for sure!

So before the second coaching session, Tejas carefully prepared his new business strategy. He took extra caution this time and presented a realistic one to his coach. This coaching session was an eye-opener for him as it provided him with a new perspective of his business strategy. Do you know what that was? He realised that he had pegged himself with the many competitors he had in his business and had arrived at his pricing strategy at those levels. By pricing at this level, Tejas had totally omitted looking at the bigger players and how he could scale up his business to the next level. Again, he realised how his priorities needed to change.

This realisation opened a totally new dimension of his business outlook, and he had an "aha" moment. He quickly started building on this area by identifying the loopholes of the bigger players, started addressing the pain points of his customers and increased his pricing levels. To his own surprise, his business grew to higher levels, and he was more than happy that he had got himself a high-performance coach.

It didn't stop there. Tejas continued his coaching session with his coach. Tejas identified another challenge his business posed for him. While the business grew, he realised that his cash flow was impacted. So he wanted to overcome this challenge in the third coaching session. And what do you think he got as his takeaway? Yet another spark of an idea. He expanded his business by opening newer verticals that were related to his main business. This happened to be his core area of strength, and in this business vertical, there were no cash flow delays. He was able to utilise the cash from this vertical to pay all the dues on time and felt a great sigh of relief. He was thrilled as well because due to the opening of the newer verticals, it contributed to the growth of his business.

WHAT YOU CAN LEARN FROM TEJAS' STORY

> ➢ *Set realistic goals, stretch as much as possible, get your priorities right and challenge yourself.*

> ➢ *Do not undermine your potential.*

> ➢ *Overexcitement can blur your vision from reality. Be mindful of it.*

In this rushed rat race world that we are living in, we often tend to become like robots and set ourselves into an automatic mode without thinking. You start doing your work, you get a ping from a friend, you check your phone, and one thing leads to another and before you realise it, 30 minutes have gone past! And this seems to repeat itself. You tell yourself that it is ok just this time and that you will fix it next time. But guess what, this has become almost a routine! As a result, you feel that you don't have enough time, and there are so many pending things to be completed. While all of them seem important, you become unsure which ones need more priority than the others. So even though you claim that your high-performance goals are a priority, they tend to take a back seat without your knowledge.

The ping from a friend is only an example. It can even be your thoughts when you start building on them further or when you intend on taking a 5-minute music break or TV break and before you realise it, the time has gone way past that. Of course, breaks are essential, but are you prolonging your break more than required? How are you getting control of this?

One of the best ways to break this chain is to pause for a moment and question yourself. Just check with yourself:

1. Are you doing the right thing?

2. Is it required now?

3. Is there an alternative way?

4. Is there anything that you can do differently?

5. Are you conscious of your time?

Therefore, the key here is "Awareness"

By increasing your awareness levels, you become more cognizant of the way you are prioritising your high-performance targets and working on them. Be conscious of what you are doing. Take a moment to pause and check with yourself.

ACTIVITY

In order to prioritise, keep a tab of your time, try this time tracker, which will enhance your awareness levels. Feel free to modify the time tracker to suit your needs. Once your awareness grows, complete the ones with higher priority first. Thereby, you can master the art of prioritising the more important tasks. Alternatively, there are many other readymade software that assist in tracking what is important (such as smartsheet, wrike, meistertask, etc.)

Time tracker (sample) (Date)	Activity completed	Comments/Scope for improvement
6 am – 7 am		
7 am – 8 am		
8 am – 9 am		
9 am – 10 am		
10 am – 11 am		
11 am – 12 pm		
12 pm – 1 pm		

1 pm – 2 pm		
2 pm – 3 pm		
3 pm – 4 pm		
4 pm – 5 pm		
5 pm – 6 pm		
6 pm – 7 pm		
7 pm – 8 pm		
8 pm – 9 pm		
9 pm – 10 pm		
10 pm – 11 pm		
11 pm – 12 am		

REFLECTION

- *What can be a good trigger for you to become more aware of prioritising whatever is important for you?*

- *What does it take for you to make or break a habit?*

- *How about retaining the essential practices as your habit and doing away with the rest?*

SUMMARY

- *Wear your thinking cap at all times.*

- *Question yourself.*

- *Enhance your awareness levels.*

Chapter 5

TURN OFF THE UNWANTED

"Shutting out the unwanted mind chatter leads you to high performance."

Uma had been an exceptionally bright student during her school and college days. She wanted to pursue her studies further, but the family's financial condition did not permit her to do so. So she commenced her working career after her graduation. After working for a few years, she had saved up for her further education. Being extremely passionate about uplifting girl children from slums, she decided to prepare to become an IAS Officer to serve the Government and enrolled herself in the course.

Soon after, cupid struck. She was head over heels in love with her colleague and wanted to be married to him. But in filmy style, her conservative parents opposed this. She did not want to go against their wishes. However, she firmly told them that if at all she got married, it would be to this particular chap. This debate ensued between her and her parents for a while. The discussion of her marriage was always a painful one with emotions ruling, not just for her but for her parents too. Whatever she spoke or did would loop back to her marriage, leaving Uma in tears.

Once the pet of her father, she was now not even on proper talking terms with him. The gifts she bought for her parents for festivals were not accepted. Because of all the drama at home, Uma started having sleepless nights. She was unable to focus on her studies. Whilst many of her friends were doing well in their career as well as managing their children, Uma felt that at 30, she was far from being successful both in her personal as well as her professional life.

With this emotional trauma, she was unable to study. She tried hard to focus and prepare for her exams, but the moment she opened her books, she would drift into her fear-filled world of either hearing abuses from her father or her mother crying to her about her bad choice of her future husband or the fear of her boyfriend abandoning her. Sometimes, even worse, she would imagine them being married but having a failed marriage.

Uma felt miserable and did not know what to do. Upon advice from her friend, she sought help from a high-performance coach. She confessed that she wanted to be an IAS officer but was unable to prepare for her exams despite being a bright student.

After a long discussion with her coach, Uma suddenly burst out into tears. The conversation with the coach helped her discover two things. One was her mind chatter due to the concern about her marriage. The second was the root cause of her fear. Her fear stemmed from the fact that she did not trust her boyfriend fully. Because her parents were not for it, she was worried if he would get impatient and let go of her.

Uma decided to have an open conversation with her boyfriend and fix the second issue. For the first issue of mind chatter, she further took her coach's help to overcome the same.

WHAT CAN YOU LEARN FROM UMA'S STORY?

➤ *Negative thoughts do not allow you to be productive.*

➤ *It is the nature of the human mind to keep chatting. Be aware of it and see how you can go beyond it.*

➤ *If you are disturbed in your personal life, it impacts your professional life.*

To achieve high performance, it is essential to minimise the unwanted mind chatter. Your mind can be your best friend and your worst enemy. It is up to you to mould your mind the way you want it.

Now that you have stated your goals and know the purpose behind it, let's move ahead.

A common challenge in the path of your high performance is your mind chatter. Research says that the average person has up to sixty thousand thoughts per day! Not only do the thoughts arise, but they also start to chatter with you, thereby distracting your performance. This hinders your potential and, therefore, your performance is not at its best.

The Inner Game of Tennis by Tim Gallwey is a book that talks about Self-1 and Self-2 that interfere with performance. The book also states that the difference between **Performance** and **Potential** is self-interference.

THE KEY IS TO FOCUS.

Keep this mind chatter and self-interference at bay, especially when you want to peak your performance potential. Each one may have different strategies to focus. What is yours? Some suggested ways that you can improve your focus levels are:

1. Create a suitable schedule.

2. Take short breaks in between.

3. Set a timer for a few minutes, during which you are focussing only on your activity.

4. Focus on your mind chatter for a few minutes and let it pass. Then get back to what you are doing.

5. Become conscious about your mind chatter but learn to ignore it.

6. Remember that the more you try to control your mind voice, the more it tends to chatter.

7. Acknowledge the chatter, but continue to do what you want to do.

8. If you still feel you are getting disturbed, focus on your breath for 30-60 seconds and then get back to what you are doing. Do it as frequently as required as it helps in reducing the mind chatter.

AVAILABILITY QUOTIENT IS ONE TRICK THAT CAN HELP YOU WITH YOUR FOCUS.

- Check if you are in the present moment. How available are you for yourself?

- How aware are you about your needs, wants and desires?

- Are you available for yourself when you need yourself the most?

- How are you nurturing your growth?

- Are you present for yourself, to do what is meaningful to you?

Keep checking on yourself regarding your availability quotient to improve your focus. You can also set a trigger or a reminder to keep a tab on your availability quotient.

Availability quotient = Time invested in focussed and productive activity or outcome for yourself/Total time taken * 100

For example, you have to submit an important and urgent report to your boss within the next 60 minutes. Let us assume the first 5 minutes are spent chatting with your colleagues about your meeting with your boss. You work for the next 15 minutes, and then you get a phone call, which takes away another 5 minutes. Again, you work for 20 minutes after which another colleague wants to discuss something not so important. You lose another five minutes there. Finally, by the 60th minute, because of the deadline, you manage to send the report to your boss, but you know that you could have done better.

Your availability quotient is 45/60 * 100 = 75%

You know that if you had an extra 10-15 minutes, the report would have been perfect, which means you need to increase your availability quotient from 75% to 100% to achieve high performance.

ACTIVITY

What can you do to ensure better focus in your area of work? Complete the table below to allow free flowing thoughts to ensure focus on your output.

My proposed ways to ensure focus on what I do:

1. _____

_____

_____

_____

_____

2. _____

_____

_____

_____

_____

3. _____

_____

_____

_____

_____

My Availability Quotient score:

Name of Activity	Time Invested	Total Time for Activity	My Score

REFLECTION

- *How can you strike a balance between focus and defocus?*

- *How can you improve your availability quotient?*

- *How can you strive to get better with your focus level?*

SUMMARY

- *Minimise mind chatter.*

- *Improve your focus.*

- *Create your strategy.*

- *Increase your availability quotient.*

Chapter 6

TRACK WHAT'S IMPORTANT

"Quit the worthless.
Pursue the worthwhile for high performance."

Tarun was an entrepreneur with many aspirations to grow his business further. He put in a lot of effort and worked for hours together, as he was driven and committed to succeeding in his business. However, the challenge his business posed on him was that while the business grew, he felt he did not have any time for himself nor his family or even manage all aspects of his business. His wife and two teenage children were unhappy with him, as he hardly got to spend any time with them. Even over dinner, he used to be on calls, think and discuss business matters, which only irritated his family further.

He discussed this issue with his coach. To his own surprise, he got amazing solutions at the end of this session. He realised that he had a fantastic team, yet he was not delegating work. He was independently handling all aspects of the business. He was actually micromanaging every aspect of the business. He realised that he was behaving like this as he did not trust his team's capabilities fully.

The coach asked him to list the reasons for the same, and Tarun realised it was only because of his ego. He thought he was superior in terms of knowledge compared to his team members. Now that the reality dawned on him, he decided to take action—to ensure that each of his team members contributed directly and that his role was more at the managerial level.

> ## WHAT CAN YOU LEARN FROM TARUN'S STORY?
>
> ➢ *It is important to balance all aspects of your life.*
>
> ➢ *Learn the art of delegation by knowing which tasks can be delegated (or outsourced).*
>
> ➢ *Success is to be measured by what you are foregoing to achieve it.*

A common deterrent for most people is *the lack of time*. You are perpetually busy. You want to do many things, and you just don't seem to find the time. *FOMO* or *Fear Of Missing Out* only makes it worse. Plus, there are also umpteen distractions, which range from social media, messaging, television, news, movies, browsing, online shopping and what not! As a result, all of these eat away into your precious time, making you feel that you do not have time for anything that you want to do, and you seem to be in a constant race against time. This lack of time also does not allow you to practice. And for high performance, you need to **keep practising until you achieve mastery and consistency.**

On the other hand, the distractions could be good as they help you to de-stress and focus better, help you in networking and conversations, improve your awareness, etc. This being the case, how can you balance the two? How would you know where to draw the line, as the distractions are a bottomless pit?

THE KEY TO MANAGING THIS IS BY PRACTISING "WORTHFULNESS" OF EACH ACTIVITY THAT YOU WANT TO DO.

How worthy is the time you are spending on each activity? Become more aware of this factor, as this will help you to become wiser in your decision making. Like how you would make a financial decision based on the return on investment, set a measure for each activity on what returns it is giving you. There is this term—*ROTI* or *Return on Time Invested*. Just because you think that time is a free resource, do not abuse it.

Here are some hacks that you can follow:

1. Parkinson's Law: Work expands to fill the time available for completion. So if you would like to manage your time better, set yourself a time frame for each activity.

2. If you would like to be more productive with your available time, set necessary criteria to measure the core of your productivity. (For example, certain outcome or desired output or enabling growth, etc.)

3. Challenge yourself. For instance, see if you can complete a particular task within 90% of the usual time you take.

4. Know how to keep distractions at bay. (Like switching off notifications on your phone while you are focussing on completion.)

5. Be more aware of the areas where your time is being invested.

6. If it helps, prepare a timesheet to track your time.

7. Set a specific time for distractions. For example, I will check my phone every two hours for 15 minutes and will not touch it in between.

8. Calculate the ROTI. Here is a formula to calculate it as a percentage.

   Time taken for an activity * 100/Available time

   Here is an example to illustrate.

   - Of the 24 hours in a day, let's say you spend 8 hours sleeping, 8 hours at work, 4 hours for routines like eating, bathing, travelling, etc.

   - This leaves you with 4 hours to do whatever you want to do.

   - And in these four hours, let's say, you want to complete two chapters of reading a book in your domain, watch a movie, browse your social media, attend an online knowledge webinar for 30 minutes, etc.

   - Suppose you spend one hour to browse your social media, then your ROTI score is:

   - 60 minutes * 100/240 minutes = 25%

   - You need to assess if you are getting 25% of your time's worth by spending it on social media or if it would be better if you spend 25% reading the two chapters of the book in your domain.

   - You need to weigh the pros and cons of each and decide what is right for you.

9. Similar to computing ROTI, you can also compute your productivity score. This can be utilised only for all the productive activities that help you with your high-performance areas.

10. Design your own hacks to maximise your available time. For example, listening to audio podcasts while driving, checking your social media while waiting for the elevator, reading a book during your travel time, etc.

ACTIVITY

Here is a sample format you can use to measure your productivity:

Activity No.	Nature of activity for high performance	Current productivity score on a scale of 10 (10 being the highest)	Targeted productivity score	Comments on how to improve the time for each activity
1				
2				
3				
4				
5				

REFLECTION

- *List your distractions. What are the possibilities you can make them contribute to your growth?*

- *How can you become more effective in utilising your time?*

- *How can you be accountable and committed with your time?*

SUMMARY

- *Keep track of your worthy activities.*

- *Work expands to fill the time available.*

- *Hacks to maximise your available time.*

- *Get better at what you do.*

Chapter 7

STEP OUT TO STEP UP

"The magic of high performance happens when you step out of your comfort zone."

A few years ago, Vikas was a champion in computer programming. He used to code and write amazing programmes. He took to programming like fish to water. He was considered one of the star performers of the organisation. Subsequently, his company was taken over by a large multinational where Vikas' role was considered redundant. The computer language he was programming had become outdated. Vikas was so engrossed in his work that he had failed to upgrade his skills.

Being thrown out of the job was a big blow to Vikas. He tried to get jobs in other organisations, but it was the same story everywhere. His skillset was outdated. He was without a job for over a year. A friend of his recommended him to a contact for a job. Vikas got the job, but the pay was very low, and the workload was high. He could not sustain in the place and was soon out a job again. He was living off his wife's salary.

His wife recommended that he study further, but he was not up to it. They would get into huge arguments because of this. He told her that even if he studied something, it would get outdated and argued with her that age was not on his side and, therefore, he would not get a job. His relatives started making fun of him, saying his name "Vikas" meant progress, but he just couldn't progress in his career. Vikas was deeply upset.

Vikas got a few interview calls but failed to perform well in them. He could not sound assertive about himself and hence was rejected in all of them. Vikas started to blame everyone around him, saying no one knew his worth. As luck would have it or, rather, as ill-luck would have it, his wife also lost her job. Soon, they were running out of funds. Their son had secured admission in a foreign university, but his education was getting affected as they could not afford the fees. Vikas was now under tremendous self-pressure to ensure the wellbeing of his family. He started having anxiety pangs.

He wanted to have a conversation with his high-performance coach. Vikas poured out his pain regarding his career and the many rejections he had faced to his heart's content. The coach listened patiently. Vikas seemed to have a strong belief that he did not want to work again as a programmer. He also didn't want to study further and didn't want a job that would underpay him compared to his last drawn salary. With these criteria that he had set for himself, it seemed quite a challenge for Vikas to progress.

The coach asked him to list down his areas of interest and what he liked to do. Vikas thought and finally said that he liked maths a lot and used to be a topper in his school and college days. He also said that he liked and was well versed with many prayers and chants. He even admitted that without the job and having too much time on his hand, he had learnt many new prayers, their meanings and could even recite a few of them by heart.

The coach probed further and asked him if there was a way to capitalise on his skills and make a new living out of it. It was a total aha moment for Vikas. While he seemed keen to venture into it, he realised that it was something he had never done. So he prepared himself to try his hands on it and step out of his comfort zone. He sprung to action immediately. He started teaching school children maths and also started conducting an online course for adults who were interested to know more about culture and spirituality.

Vikas had stepped out of his comfort zone and thus succeeded in rebuilding his career.

WHAT CAN YOU LEARN FROM VIKAS' STORY?

➢ *When you indulge in activities that you like, you do not feel the stress of doing it as compared to doing a task that you dislike.*

➢ *It is essential to reinvent yourself in line with the changing times.*

➢ *Your hobbies and interests have the potential to be another revenue stream for you.*

It is said that magic happens outside the comfort zone. Yet you feel so happy and cosy when snuggled inside your comfort zone, only doing whatever you are comfortable with. But only if you do stuff that you are not used to, stuff that is different, can you expect different results. **Same actions will only yield the same results.** The thought of taking extra pains to step outside your comfort zone seems to challenge you.

While you may want to do it, there is always a "but" that is stopping you from stepping out.

If you want to achieve that extra bit and go the extra mile, for you to accomplish your goals, then check with yourself if it would help you to step out of your comfort zone. Doing the same things each time will only give you the same results. What are you doing differently to get to your set goals?

You need to create your set of "superset", which could help you to step out of your comfort zone. They are offset, reset, onset, mindset, skillset, asset and subset. Let me share a little more about each of these.

1. Offset – Offset your negative thoughts with positive ones. Use whatever motivates you.

2. Reset – Press your reset button to start afresh, leaving aside the old thoughts and your older version.

3. Onset – Turn on and tune in your thoughts to sync in with the reality of what you want to achieve.

4. Mindset – You need to adopt the right mindset that will aid you to step out of your comfort zone.

5. Skillset – Upskill yourself in the area where you want to achieve high performance. Reach out to the experts, mentors, advisers, coaches, etc. to sharpen your skillsets.

6. Asset – Asset, here, refers to your knowledge, skill levels, expertise, etc. Adopt an asset-building thought process, which you can leverage on, for your growth.

7. Subset – If you need to break down the steps to step out of your comfort zone, break them into smaller subsets and follow the above steps.

THE KEY IS TO STEP OUT OF YOUR COMFORT ZONE IS WHAT I CALL "BLISSCIPLINE", WHICH IS A COMBINATION OF BLISS PLUS DISCIPLINE.

Get familiar and make yourself comfortable with the particular activity so that you get a feeling of bliss. Once you reach that level, ensure that you get it into the habit of making it a discipline. This is blisscipline.

By adopting blisscipline, what you are actually doing is expanding your comfort zone. So you still feel that you are within your comfort zone, and yet, your capabilities have increased.

ACTIVITY

List the steps required for you to step out of your comfort zone in your selected domain of high performance and, thereafter, expand your comfort zone.

Suggestion

If it would help, start with areas that you are passionate about.

1. _____

_____

_____

2. _____

_____

_____

3. _____

_____

_____

4. _____

_____

_____

5. _____

_____

_____

REFLECTION

- *What benefits do you foresee by stepping out of your comfort zone that will help you achieve high performance?*

- *What are the excuses you are giving yourself that prevent you from stepping out of your comfort zone?*

- *What can act as a trigger for you to ensure that you are stepping out of your comfort zone until you make it a habit?*

SUMMARY

- *Magic happens outside your comfort zone.*

- *Create bliss + discipline.*

- *Expand your comfort zone.*

Chapter 8

ART OF SELF-MANAGEMENT

"Master the art of energy management for high performance."

Nandan was an extremely successful and popular businessman in his city. His reach was wide, and he had a very good network, not just within his city but throughout the country. Nandan was hard-working, efficient as well as a shrewd person. Because of his popularity, Nandan was involved in many business forums. He was elected as the president in two of the forums and was the board of director in three other forums. Apart from these, Nandan managed two of his large businesses. He also had many goals for himself in the areas of self-development and philanthropy. On his personal front, he aspired to author books and wanted to spend more time with his ageing parents and young children.

In most of the forums that Nandan was part of, there were ego clashes, backbiting and finger-pointing between other members. In such cases, Nandan was called upon to mediate between the parties. Nandan enjoyed the fact that the others looked upon him for solutions not only in these clashes but also for their business issues. Nandan rejoiced at the limelight and the respect he gained from the fellow business folks.

Nandan had set himself many targets and wanted to achieve many things, both professionally and personally. However, he felt he was not progressing at the pace he wanted to and was dejected with himself. Given the many roles and responsibilities he had, there were umpteen tasks that he had to complete. He felt overwhelmed and did not know how to go about them. These factors only made Nandan feel stressed and did not permit him to focus. He did not know what to do. Nandan decided to have a conversation with his coach.

As the conversation with his high-performance coach progressed, Nandan realised that he was handling more than he could chew. He understood that he had to prioritise his tasks. He decided to let go of or postpone a few tasks as he did not want to feel overly pressurised. His biggest takeaway was he did not know how to say no. If anyone approached him for a solution, Nandan got sucked into the issue. This drained him of both his time and energy, resulting in him being unable to complete what was important for him.

The coach probed further on what else was causing the drain. It dawned on Nandan that what added fuel to the situation was the underlying mental and emotional drain that was caused by his business rival. When the coach asked him how it served him, Nandan realised that it did no good to him. He immediately started working on himself to change his attitude and perspective. This helped him ease his stress levels. The coach asked him how he was planning to de-stress. That was when he felt the need to de-stress. He started practising meditation regularly, which helped him tremendously.

Nandan was back on track again on the path of high performance.

WHAT CAN YOU LEARN FROM NANDAN'S STORY?

➢ *Don't bite off more than you can chew. You can always postpone doing certain things to a later date.*

➢ *It is easy to get stressed but important to de-stress.*

➢ *Learn to say no to tasks that do not enrich you.*

In the present times, what is one common thing among kids, teens, adults and the aged? **Stress!** Stress seems to be an integral part of many people's lives. While a little amount of stress or pressure may do us good, the stress levels are invariably huge that it impacts not only performance levels but also health.

And the best way to beat stress is to de-stress! How does one de-stress? Whatever works well for you. It could be movies, music, shopping, chatting with a dear one, cooking, painting, meditation, etc. You must ensure that you do something about the stress and get over it. Living with high stress levels is not going to do you any good. So, just chill!

Some common reasons for stress are caused by an inability to handle:

- Situation
- Relationships
- Emotions
- Anxiety

What are your thoughts around stress? Do you even realise when you get stressed? Have you thought what triggers your stress? Does the best in you come out with high levels of stress?

Further, when we are stressed about something, it obstructs other related areas. For example, if you are stressed about a particular situation at work, then you tend to take it out in your relationship, which only ruins your relationship. Therefore, keeping stress at bay is the best. It could be easier said than done. However, by taking charge of yourself consciously, you can make it work.

THE KEY TO HANDLING STRESS IS ENERGY MANAGEMENT

Simply stated, learning to manage your energies will help you combat stress better. Do not spend your energy on unwanted things. Likewise, unwanted thoughts also drain you. Instead, you can use this energy during the times you are stressed, and it will help you get over your stress faster. Like, for instance, if you use up your energy in too much gossip or backbiting or rumour-mongering, it would only drain you further. See what energises you. For example, it could be a power distraction or power recreation (similar to a power nap) in between your focussed work. Likewise, if you are sleep deprived, you will not have sufficient energy levels to handle stress.

According to Sri Sri Ravi Shankar, the spiritual guru and the founder of "The Art of Living", there are four sources of energy. They are food, sleep, breadth and meditative state of mind. So see how you can work on gaining the most from each of these sources and, at the same time, learn to conserve your energy. Utilise your energy wisely.

ACTIVITY

Fill in your stress table as below:

Situations that usually cause me stress:	Relationships that usually increase my stress:
1. _____	1. _____
_____	_____
_____	_____
2. _____	2. _____
_____	_____
_____	_____
3. _____	3. _____
_____	_____
Emotions that usually arouse my stress levels:	What am I anxious about that causes me stress?
1. _____	1. _____
_____	_____
_____	_____
2. _____	2. _____
_____	_____
_____	_____
3. _____	3. _____
_____	_____
_____	_____

Now fill in your de-stress table as below:

When stressed by situations, I will	When stressed by relationships, I will
1. _____	1. _____
_____	_____
_____	_____
2. _____	2. _____
_____	_____
_____	_____
3. _____	3. _____
_____	_____
_____	_____
When stressed by my emotions, I will	When I am anxious, I will de-stress by
1. _____	1. _____
_____	_____
_____	_____
2. _____	2. _____
_____	_____
_____	_____
3. _____	3. _____
_____	_____
_____	_____

REFLECTION

- *How will you know when you are stressed?*

- *How does getting stressed help you in your high-performance goal?*

- *Is there a way you can de-stress quickly?*

SUMMARY

- *It is essential to de-stress.*

- *Manage your energy.*

- *Switch between focussed sessions and power distractions.*

Chapter 9

OVERCOMING FEARS

"Chuck the fear of failure if you seek high performance."

Gaurav had just turned thirty and was doing fine in his career. Life took an unexpected U-turn after he had a road accident. His legs were permanently damaged due to the impact of the accident, and he was unable to be mobile like before. This became a huge setback for him—more mentally than physically. The initial days were hell for Gaurav. The thought that he had to be dependent on someone for every little thing, to move, being unable to play his favourite game of badminton, inability to hang out with his friends and so on made Gaurav feel depressed. He wondered how he would cope for the rest of his life.

After a few weeks, Gaurav started getting used to the new way of his life. He started to heal physically. However, the doctors had told him that his legs would never be the same. This made Gaurav get into his cocoon, and he became very anxious about his future. Who would want to marry him? Being the only son, who could he even reach out to for support? He felt his life was doomed. He cried to himself.

A few months later, a friend of his connected him with an association of people with disabilities. The association also offered jobs or connected with organisations for people with disabilities. Gaurav saw many others whose plight was much worse than his. He also witnessed how a few people had changed their course of life despite their disabilities. They were mentally strong and were making a change in society in various possible ways. Gaurav felt extremely inspired. He wanted to take charge of his life again and determine the best possible action he needed to take to propel himself ahead. He felt hopeful that his life could blossom again.

Gaurav started thinking about what he could possibly do and get ahead. He wanted to discuss it with his high-performance coach. During the course of the conversation, what emerged strongly for Gaurav was he did not want to be in employment. He was firm that he wanted to be an employer. So together with the coach, they deep dived into the areas of his interest and what he could manage despite his disability. After shortlisting the possibilities, Gaurav began to evaluate each option, and he was ready to get started right away. He launched his business successfully, which involved other people with disabilities.

Gaurav now began earning more than he did at his last job at the time of the accident. Gaurav felt satisfied and accomplished that despite his disabilities, he could do well in business and also provide opportunities to other people with disabilities.

He still had his fears in his personal life about getting a life partner but decided to accept the reality and move on further.

WHAT CAN YOU LEARN FROM GAURAV'S STORY?

➢ *Despite unexpected setbacks in life, explore possibilities to move ahead.*

➢ *Seek inspiration and get inspired.*

➢ *It is alright to have your fears, but it is important to accept them.*

FEAR OF FAILURE IS ONE OF THE BIGGEST FACTORS THAT PLAYS UP ON YOUR PERFORMANCE

You probably want to try your hands at many new things or maybe even want to put on a performance to an audience or speak in public, but it is the fear of failure that blocks you. It further worsens when you think *"Oh! What will people say?!"* and these thoughts do not encourage you and only pull you down.

If this feeling resonates with you, then just remember that there is a first time for everything. Remember how you struggled as a child to take the first step? You fumbled. You fell down. But did it stop you from trying again? Did you give up then? So what is different now?

I would also urge you to think and reflect what is causing this fear, and what it is doing to you. Where is the fear stemming from? How is this fear serving your growth?

THE SECRET KEY TO OVERCOMING THE FEAR OF FAILURE IS GRIT

Apart from the meaning of the word *grit*, it also stands for

- G – Gear up
- R – Rise up
- I – Idealise
- T – Thrive

So here is how you can go about it:

1. Gear up by preparing yourself mentally. Be prepared to do whatever it takes to accomplish what you want.

2. Rise to the occasion by standing up for yourself and your dreams. Let go of the past. Think of this as a new beginning.

3. Idealise the perfect outcome that you desire and see what it needs to be to get to that result.

4. Thrive on your ideas. Thrive on abundance. Thrive on implementation.

Therefore, determine what you need to aim for, which can motivate you to overcome the fear of failure.

Apart from the above, you could also:

1. Ensure that you are self-motivated.

2. Say positive things about yourself and your goals.

3. Look for inspiration and be inspired.

4. Have a contingency plan in place.

5. Do not be afraid to try again.

With regard to "What will others say?", others will always say something or the other. If you have gained weight, they will say, "Have you been eating too much?" or "Are you not exercising these days?"

And if you lose weight, it would be "Are you not eating well?" or "Are your sick?" or "Have you been stressed or worried about something?" So anything that you do, "they" want to acknowledge it and share their views on it. So just let them talk. These are people who hardly matter to you and may not even stand by you at the most needed times. So why bother? You move on and do what you want to do. And, of course, people's memories are short-lived! At the end of the day, it is your life, and you live it the way you want to. Prioritise yourself and your dreams.

ACTIVITY

Complete this GRIT matrix to state your plan of action to overcome the fear of failure.

Gear up	Rise up
1. _____	1. _____
_____	_____
_____	_____
2. _____	2. _____
_____	_____
_____	_____
3. _____	3. _____
_____	_____
_____	_____
Idealise	**Thrive**
1. _____	1. _____
_____	_____
_____	_____
2. _____	2. _____
_____	_____
_____	_____
3. _____	3. _____
_____	_____
_____	_____

REFLECTION

- *What happens if you fail? How will you handle it?*

- *What will encourage you to pursue despite the fear of failure?*

- *How does the fear of failure serve you in your high-performance journey?*

SUMMARY

- *Fear of failure does not allow you to do your best.*

- *Just try. There's a first time for everything.*

- *Develop GRIT.*

- *Prioritise what is important for you.*

Chapter 10

MASTER WHAT YOU LIKE

"Play on your strengths for high performance."

"Are leaders born or made?" is a common debatable topic. Irrespective of that, every leader wants to be a good leader, and every aspiring leader wants to grow their leadership skills.

There was a set of senior leaders from the CXO club who were no different. They were wondering how they could become better leaders of their teams, be good role models and become more efficient as leaders. The participants of this high-performance coaching workshop were all senior leaders from different organisations, with a common objective of getting better as leaders. What transpired at the end of the session were some valuable learnings for all the leaders. If you are a leader wanting to grow further, or an aspiring leader, this will be of interest to you.

HERE IS WHAT YOU CAN LEARN FROM THE OUTCOME OF THE WORKSHOP

➢ Listening skills – The leaders acknowledged that they were not listening fully to their team members. They also felt they had a preconceived notion, which, at times, prevented them from paying full attention to the words of their teammates. So, they wanted to work on improving their listening skills.

➢ Appreciation – They felt that the important point for immediate action was that, as leaders, they needed to appreciate and encourage their team members. By lacking words of appreciation, they felt they were depriving their team of recognition and motivation. So appreciation was an implementable action these leaders walked away with.

➢ Attitude to Learning – Upon reflection, they realised that leaders need to be open to learning from all, including their juniors. At times, the fact that they were senior subconsciously prevented them from learning from their juniors. They wanted to do away with the "know it all" attitude as it came in the way of their new learnings. It dawned on them that it impacted their learning negatively, which they decided to set right.

➢ Ego – The fourth valuable insight they got was, as leaders, they felt they needed to let go of their ego. They had high expectations that their team needed to follow their instructions and not challenge them about their decisions as they were senior in position compared to their teammates. At the end of the session, the leaders realised that they should let go of their ego.

> ➤ Mindfulness – They felt that, as leaders, they needed to strive to be mindful of their words and actions—as leaders have the responsibility of leading by example. Thus, they got greater awareness that they had to be careful with their words, behaviour and actions. They decided to exhibit caution in their approach so that their team could follow suit.

The leaders were happy with this newfound awareness. While some of the points were easy to adapt to, they realised that some of them were challenging, given their personality types. Some of the participants decided to inculcate in their leadership style, their shortcomings that they would overcome. The rest decided to leverage their strengths to make the most of their leadership abilities. Leaders also need to be coached on improving their leadership skills as that helps them to bring out the best leader in them. The leaders were extremely happy with their takeaways. They felt ready to take on their teams.

Each of us has our own tastes, preferences and strengths. Similarly, we have our own share of compulsion, dislikes and weaknesses. We prefer to do what we like and procrastinate what we dislike. There are times you don't even realise that you don't want to do something simply only because it is something that does not interest you or maybe you do not find value in it. You may push yourself to do what you dislike, but unless there is a compelling reason or a deadline, you never go about completing it.

This is a normal human trait. The crucial part here is to evaluate if there is a way you can bypass and get away by not doing what you dislike. Indeed, there is not much choice with the essential ones. For instance, if you do not like to brush your teeth daily, you do not have a choice but to do so! But imagine if there was a way to get away with the stuff that you dislike (or your weakness) that forms part of your high-performance goal.

Let me give you an example. After about two decades of working experience in various corporates in the field of marketing, Sanjay wanted to become an independent marketing consultant. His mentor advised that for Sanjay to start off on his own, he needed to prove his authority on the subject that would help him in getting clients. According to his mentor, Sanjay could prove his expertise in marketing by writing books, blogs, speaking in forums, podcasts, videos, etc. While Sanjay agreed with his mentors' views, Sanjay disliked speaking in public, and the idea of podcasts and videos also did not resonate with him. However, Sanjay was a prolific writer. He published a couple of marketing books and also regularly wrote marketing articles for magazines and other media which gained a lot of traction, thereby getting him many clients. He never spoke at forums, nor did he get into the space of videos and podcasts.

So what did Sanjay do? **THE KEY IS HE "LEVERAGED" ON HIS STRENGTHS.**

Sanjay got away by not indulging in areas that were not his preference. And by leveraging on his strengths, he got closer to his professional high-performance goals.

Thus, concerning preferences in connection with your high-performance goals, you could segregate them as:

1. Should do's

2. Your strengths

3. Your dislikes

4. Eliminate unwanted tasks

One other point you must remember is, you are constantly evolving, and so are your tastes and preferences. So something that you dislike now could probably become something that you get around to liking later on. So it is not bad to think that you can also work around converting your dislikes into your likes, especially if it works to your advantage.

This would give you a good idea of what you should do and how you can leverage your strengths so that you can play around with them.

ACTIVITY

Complete this matrix to leverage your strengths

Should do	Key strengths/preferences
1. _____ _____ _____ 2. _____ _____ _____ 3. _____ _____ _____	1. _____ _____ _____ 2. _____ _____ _____ 3. _____ _____ _____
My weakness/dislikes	**Eliminate**
1. _____ _____ _____ 2. _____ _____ _____ 3. _____ _____ _____	1. _____ _____ _____ 2. _____ _____ _____ 3. _____ _____ _____

REFLECTION

- *Is there a way you can convert your dislikes into your likes?*

- *What is the best way to leverage your strengths to achieve your high-performance goal?*

- *What are the unwanted tasks that you can eliminate?*

SUMMARY

- *Each of us has our own taste and preferences, which need to be respected.*

- *Find a loophole and make a cheat sheet to get away with stuff you dislike.*

- *Leverage your positives.*

Chapter 11

GET REAL

"Have the right mindset to be in the high-performance zone."

Deepak was an IT professional with around 13 years of working experience. He was overwhelmed with work. On average, he used to clock in about 12 hours a day for the organisation where he worked. At a recent family gathering, he realised that most of his cousins were in senior positions in the corporate world, compared to him. While he was happy about their progress, he felt low about himself and felt the need to fast track his career to be on par with the rest. This meant he had to upskill himself and probably study further.

But he felt confused and was not sure what the right course for him to pursue would be. Deepak also realised that he actually did not have time for his career development. He further felt that he should get promoted in his current organisation, considering all the hard work he put in. However, when he spoke to his boss about his promotion, his boss pointed out areas where he had to improve before climbing the corporate ladder. This included his communication skills and time management skills, which were a deterrent to his promotion.

Deepak felt demotivated, hearing this from his boss. He started feeling anxious about his future.

Deepak had yet another concern too. At the family gathering, some of his relatives commented jokingly how Deepak seemed older than his real age because of his potbelly and grey hair. Although Deepak didn't react to them, deep down, he felt hurt hearing that. He wanted to work out and reduce his belly and get back into proper shape. But then, where could he find the time, he wondered.

It was at this juncture that he decided to seek the services of a high-performance coach, which proved to be a game-changer for Deepak. The coach deep dived into the root cause, which helped Deepak to overcome his beliefs about himself. The reality that appeared to Deepak was, deep down, he had a huge inferiority complex, and hence, even though he knew everything about the work that he did, he was being doubly cautious to ensure he was doing his work correctly. And this is what had impacted both his communication as well as his time management. He was actually thinking twice before he could answer and, therefore, the flow of words was not smooth, resulting in lack of cogency. Further, he realised that he was spending too much time checking all his work, which resulted in spending extra hours in the office.

During the coaching conversation, it transpired to Deepak that he just had to let go of his inferiority complex, which would enable him to be the subject matter expert. He knew that if he could let go of it, his life would transform for the better. Hence he resorted to programming his mind in such a way that he could succeed.

He went to on realise that by doing so, he would not have to spend long hours at work and utilise that time to learn and upgrade his skills, which would help him in his career growth. He decided to talk to his seniors about the right courses to pursue, which would help him acquire more knowledge in his area of work. The extra time he would get now would also help him find time for working out. He felt confident and empowered with his newfound insights. He also knew that he could peak his potential and was ready to get to greater heights. Deepak is now extremely happy with his career progression.

What you can learn from Deepak's story

- *You don't have to wait till others start pointing out your flaws. You can get started right away.*

- *Learn to manage your time and communication efficiently.*

- *Feeling inferior (or superior) can be a hurdle in the path of your progress.*

The kind of attitude you adopt towards your high-performance goals matters in accomplishing them. Knowingly or unknowingly, you could be telling yourself stories about what you want to achieve. These stories can either help you achieve or can pull you down, depending on the way your mind perceives and absorbs the story. The words that you tell yourself form the basis of the behaviour and attitude that you develop.

The positive stories you are telling yourself could be that *you want to*, *you have to* and *you can* achieve your goal. These build confidence in your subconscious mind. The negative stories are the opposite ones that tell you that *you are not meant for it, you are not capable, it is difficult* and that *you cannot.*

There are times when the negative stories may do good too. One is because it is for you to judge and make the right decision. (For example, if you were asked to jump off from the first floor of a building, what your mind tells you is you cannot do it as it is not good for you. So you need to take the right decision based on your judgement). Two, it also helps you to question yourself and your preconceived notions on whether it is something that you can actually do or not, thereby making you challenge yourself and then take the right decision for you in each circumstance.

THE KEY TO OVERCOME THIS NEGATIVE ATTITUDE IS "MIND PROGRAMME"

Based on the judgement you arrive at, if it is something that you want to proceed with, if it is something that is good for you and helps in your growth, all you have to do is it programme your mind—just like a software program. The code you have to write for your mind is the positivity, motivation and determination. Convince yourself that it is possible to achieve what you want. Believe in yourself. And, most importantly, be real on what you want and how you are planning to go about it.

If you feel you are too caught up with your negative stories, rewire and reprogramme your mind to tell you only the positive and encouraging stories so that you can get the right attitude and move forward in the path of high performance.

ACTIVITY

Think about the stories that you are telling yourself. Also, state if it is a positive story or otherwise. List them under each relevant area:

1. Stories on my capabilities

_____

_____

_____

_____

2. Stories on my wants, desires and dreams

_____

_____

_____

_____

3. Stories on why I cannot make it

_____

_____

_____

_____

If you would like to deep dive further on your beliefs and attitudes, you can draw the root cause tree diagram as illustrated below, which could help you get to the root cause of the challenges that come in the way of your high performance. A sample diagram is given below. Use it to deep dive into your causes.

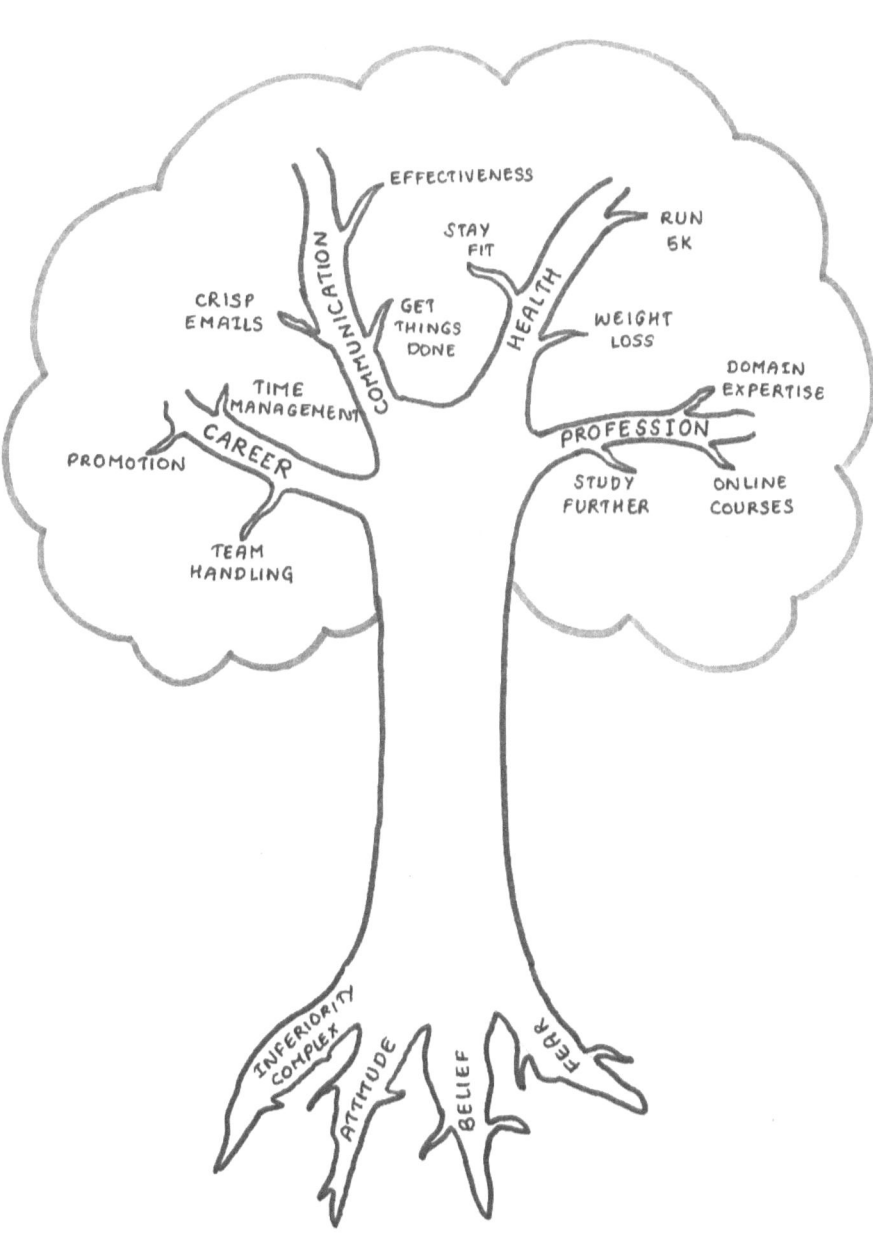

REFLECTION

- *How are the stories you are telling yourself contributing to your wellbeing?*

- *What hacks can you adopt to tell yourself encouraging stories?*

- *What are the best ways to programme your mind, which you can follow to accomplish your high-performance goals?*

SUMMARY

- *Be aware of the stories you are telling yourself.*

- *Programme your mind according to your requirement.*

- *Imbibe the right attitude to move ahead.*

Chapter 12

WHAT NEXT?

*"Set your aspirations on
high performance in all walks of your life."*

By now, I suppose you would have mastered the art of high performance. Congratulations!

There are possibilities that you might have faced some specific challenges along the path. Well, that is normal. But I will tell you what could possibly be done to navigate your way around it.

An external coach can be a good supplement to your self-coaching journey. You may wonder why an external coach. Let me share with you. Like you already know, by self-coaching, you can:

- Learn and perform
- Manage self-interference
- Be your guiding force
- Be independent of others

What you could miss out while coaching yourself are:

- No different perspective
- No one to hold the mirror for you
- Lack of varied ideas to kindle your thoughts
- Nobody to challenge you
- Miss having a sounding board

An external coach is the one who can offer the above for you. Read this anecdote about a fiercely independent and career-aggressive senior professional. Over the years, Simran felt that she was lacking focus and aggressiveness in her performance and, thereby, performance in her career was lagging. She wanted to get back to her previous sharp qualities but was telling herself that age was playing up on her. She convinced herself that it was her laziness and lack of willingness to put in the efforts that resulted in her not being able to accomplish much in her career. Simran was unable to get beyond this and was stagnating.

The coach challenged her beliefs. The reality that emerged to her was that Simran was taking refuge under the pretext of age and being lazy. The fact was that she was worried if the previous stress levels and pangs of anxiety would re-enter her life and throw her work-life balance out of proportion like in the past. After long conversations with the coach and reflecting deeply on her thoughts, Simran finally decided that at this point in time, she would take the middle path and not set herself such high and over-ambitious targets.

Thus, by having an external coach, you get challenged, and the perceptions are beyond what you think. As the external coach also holds the mirror for you, it allows you to see your own shortcomings, blind spots or flaws. What did you learn from Simran's story? Reflect and check if you are hiding under any such pretexts.

The book *The Trillion Dollar Coach* that is co-authored by the big wigs of the Silicon Valley (Eric Schmidt, Jonathan Rosenberg, Alan Eagle, etc.) is written about the late Bill Campbell who has coached many leaders such as Sundar Pitchai, Shreyl Sandberg, Susan Wojcicki, Tim Cook, etc. It highlights the role played by Bill in shaping these leaders. If you would like to know more about how an external coach can contribute to your growth, mould you and provoke your creative thoughts, this book can give you that clarity. A coach inspires you and maximises your personal and professional potential.

Let me share an interesting titbit. Did you know how the word "coach" came into existence? It originated from the word "coach", a mode of transport, which is meant to take you from where you are to where you want to be. This is precisely what a coach does—helps you to get to the higher level of performance that you want. I would recommend you to try both and see what works well for you.

If you are considering working with an external coach who can lead you to high performance, are you now thinking on what basis you should select a coach? Let me tell you how. Choosing the right coach is rather simple. Just ask yourself these simple questions:

1. Do you think you can establish chemistry with your prospective coach?

2. Do you feel comfortable and at ease to talk to the person you are considering as your coach?

3. What is your gut feeling telling you about how your prospective coach can help you with your challenges?

You can further check if:

1. The person is a credentialed coach

2. What their coaching experience is and

3. Seek testimony from their clients.

High-Performance Coaching is a beautiful journey and not a destination. Did you know that people like Steve Jobs, Bill Gates, Larry Page, Oprah Winfrey, etc. worked with a coach? Also, just like how all the sports professionals have a coach to get better, everyone requires a coach to develop and bring out the best. No wonder it is said, "**Everyone needs a coach**".

That is because a coach can

- Help you fast track your progress

- Challenge you

- Give you a different perspective

- Hold you accountable

- Partner with you to bounce off your thoughts and ideas

The aspiration to achieve, combined with the awareness of possibilities, can change everything. If the persons being coached aspire to get to higher levels of performance, a coach can create the required magic. A coach is a confidant, does not judge you and only considers your potential.

Group coaching sessions are also effective. How group coaching works?

For effective group coaching, there should be a common objective to achieve as a team. Here is an example. An

American company wanted to enhance the performance levels of the teams to achieve their yearly targets. A majority of the team had been in the system for over eight years and were familiar with all the processes. The management felt that the team had reached a saturation point with regard to their performance and wondered how they could increase the teams' productivity. That was when they requested the high-performance coach to conduct a workshop for them.

The workshop was conducted. It emphasised on their business values. The members of the workshop included everyone across the organisation. The workshop was customised in such a manner that it was fun and involved learning, along with animated and exciting discussions among the members. The teams came together, and a sense of bonding was developed. It also opened the team to a deeper understanding of the company's vision and values.

The teams went a step ahead and realised how by implementing the values and the visions of the business, they would be able to deliver higher and better quality. All the participants went back with a higher state of resourcefulness, waiting to implement all their learnings from the workshop. Thus, an external coach's perspective can be effective for groups too.

Sharing another incident on how external coach helps in giving a different perspective and in holding the mirror.

In my own mission to help entrepreneurs achieve financial wellness, a successful tech entrepreneur wanted to know if I knew suitable investors for the business. Having spoken and helped many entrepreneurs, I sensed that there was something more than this the entrepreneur was seeking. The eyes showed a sense of pain and the voice had despair. Being a coach, I started probing deeper.

As the conversation progressed, the entrepreneur revealed the truth—he sought an investor because of persistent cash flow issues. The entrepreneur admitted that despite running a successful business for the past decade, cash flow was an issue month after month, and the entrepreneur wondered how to pay salaries on time.

It was disturbing emotionally as well, as this issue could not be discussed with the spouse, children, employees, or friends. Finally, the entrepreneur poured out the issues to his heart's content and felt much lighter. Being a techie, the entrepreneur admitted that there was no attention to business finance.

I realised the entrepreneur was falling prey to what I call the **"fake stake syndrome"**. Where the entrepreneur hopes that with the investment coming in, all cash flow issues will vanish permanently, without addressing the root cause of the issue. As our coaching conversation progressed, many ideas were uncovered to fix the cash flow issues. The discussions made the entrepreneur realise—

- That a new investor would only solve the cash flow issue temporarily.

- What needed to be fixed was a better system of working capital management.

- The revenue model was not right.

Do check if you are by any chance caught in any such fake stake syndrome that is unknown to you.

Therefore, evaluate what kind of coaching would work well for you. Maybe you can even consider a mix of self-coaching in certain areas and having an external coach in other areas where you need more support.

Regarding mastering your high-performance journey, here are some bonus pointers to keep you on the path of high performance.

1. Take a call on what activities are essential for you. Adopt essentialism into your life.

2. Remind yourself that practice makes perfect. Consistency is the key.

3. You have to believe in yourself.

4. I am often asked if multitasking helps. Try it for yourself and let me know whether it has helped you or not. In my opinion, it depends on what tasks you are clubbing together.

5. Know what you will have to forego by being in the path of high performance (e.g. extra hours of sleep, minimal entertainment time, letting go of non-meaningful, toxic relationships, etc.). Are you ready for it?

6. For different results, you need to think differently and do differently.

7. Nourish your body, mind and soul. It's important to nourish your mind, body and soul for best results. For example, exercise is for the body, activities are for the mind and yoga and meditation for the soul. What works for you?

8. Be relevant to the changing times.

9. You are the benchmark for yourself. Out beat yourself every time.

10. Watch out for any attention deficiency syndrome as it will not bring out your best.

11. Set yourself targets that are meaningful to you.

12. Keep a constant tab of the direction that you are headed in.

13. Turn setbacks into learning experiences.

Now, let's have some fun! Here's an interesting way to challenge yourself, improve and ensure you are on the path of high performance.

STEPS

1. Each day, pick any number from 0 to 99.

2. In the table below, the horizontal numbers represent the ones, and the vertical represents the tens.

3. So let's say you pick the number 25, the activity you have to do for that day regarding your high-performance goal would be to "*Challenge yourself*".

4. The same number cannot be picked within 100 days.

5. The idea is, in 100 days, you would have done 100 different things to up your game.

6. Get started. Take your number pick. Or ask someone else to choose for you.

7. Repeat till you complete all the 100 boxes.

	0	1	2	3	4	5	6	7	8	9
0	Reflect on the purposefulness of your high performance.	Discard the stories you are telling yourself.	Do what it takes to energise yourself.	Step out of your comfort zone.	Visualise success in your goals.	Focus on your Action goal 1.2 (Page 30).	Crush your self-doubts.	Be more available to yourself.	Keep a tab on your awareness levels.	Channelise your thoughts.
1	Strengthen your strengths.	De-stress yourself. Chill out.	Be in the now.	Throw away non-essential thoughts.	Feel enthusiastic about your goals.	Make yourself accountable and committed.	Prepare milestones of your goals.	Celebrate yourself.	Focus on Action goal 2.1 (Page 30).	Identify your role models.
2	Motivate yourself.	Come up with 3 quick ways for your goal.	Your pick to choose what you want to do today.	Surprise yourself by doing something new.	Focus on Action goal 3.2 (Page 30).	Challenge yourself.	Journal your learnings on your goal.	Check on the root cause of your mental challenges.	Connect with a coach.	Talk to your mentor.
3	Create an opportunity for yourself to prove your ability.	Give yourself some good advice.	Package your messaging effectively.	Today, you have a choice to make it count.	Listen to your mind chatter.	Strategize the path ahead.	Focus on Action goal 3.1 (Page 30).	Set a specific time each day to focus on your goal.	Increase your productivity today.	Pivot on your favourite activity.

	0	1	2	3	4	5	6	7	8	9
4	Watch your breath for 5 minutes.	Focus on action goal 3.3 (Page 30).	Learn something new about your goal.	List activities that empower your goals.	Think about your driving force.	Nurture positive thoughts.	Question yourself on performance.	List your steps to mastery.	State your next milestone.	Know your weakness.
5	Network with your domain experts.	Act on your learnings where you could have done better.	Design your next steps.	Focus on action goal 2.2 (Page 30).	Identify things and people you can seek inspiration from.	Tutor a novice in your domain.	List the possibilities to speed up your work.	Try something different on your high-performance goal.	Answer your why regarding your goal.	Give yourself a pep talk.
6	Be more mindful of your actions about your goal.	Delegate whatever tasks possible.	Focus on Action goal 2.3 (Page 30).	Allocate a laser focussed 30 minutes for goal actioning.	Set yourself a specific target for today.	Self-coach on an area of your choice.	Do away with your excuses.	Be assertive to your self.	Collate your thoughts on your goals.	Just chill – go for a long walk and reflect on your plans.
7	List your limiting beliefs.	Do what it takes to up your game.	Talk to someone with whom you can bounce your ideas.	Think about the expectations you have set for yourself.	Talk to yourself in the mirror and encourage your performance.	Write a note of improvement to yourself.	Reach out to an expert who can help you with your goals.	Break your monotony by trying something new.	Focus on Action goal 1.1 (Page 30).	Write about your fear of failure.

	0	1	2	3	4	5	6	7	8	9
8	Make notes of your unwanted thoughts.	Meditate for 15 minutes.	Practice till perfect.	Think of different ways you can succeed in your goal.	Ask 3 people who know you well to list your blind spots.	Read about something that will take you closer to your goal.	Plan your next steps.	List what you value.	Expand your comfort zone.	Find your tribe.
9	Target to improve your efficiency.	Focus on your activity for 30 minutes and defocus for 5 minutes. Repeat.	Increase your efficiency levels.	Flaunt your achievements in your mind or write it down.	Hear your inner voice and nurture it.	Focus on Action goal 1.3 (Page 30).	Welcome suggestions for improvement from your well-wishers.	Write an article summarising your high-performance journey.	Reward yourself suitably on your progress.	Self-Appraisal of your performance from the time you started.

So, once you have achieved your high-performance goals and gained mastery, what's next on your agenda?! Where do you want to head out next? What next would you like to achieve?

Remember that high performance is not only a sprint but also a marathon. A sprint because there are times you need to act quick and a marathon because it is for life. Because you are continuously evolving and striving to be a better version of you. And yes, it is never too late to start your journey of high performance. Just take it on.

For being such a wonderful reader, I bow to you and say **NAMASTE**. Here's a gift for you for completing this book. Guess what?! You can take this gift with you and use it whenever required. It is a checklist, which you can use whenever you are self-coaching. Just remember to check on these words so that you are on track for high performance.

N – Notice your thoughts

A – Awareness of your feelings

M – Measure your progress

A – Actions you need to take

S – Sense your energy level

T – Trust yourself

E – Explore possibilities

If you would like any of your other friends, family or colleagues to benefit from this book like you, do recommend this book to them so that they can also be on the path of high performance, just like you.

Connect with me – You can write to me or inbox me on social media on how you have succeeded in your journey, your most effective high-performance strategies, what worked well for you and what didn't! I look forward to getting to know about your journey.

Wishing you the best of high performance in all walks of your life.

REFLECTIONS ON MY HIGH PERFORMANCE JOURNEY – WHAT I HAVE ACHIEVED

REFLECTIONS ON MY HIGH PERFORMANCE JOURNEY – WHAT I LEARNT ABOUT MYSELF

www.ingramcontent.com/pod-product-compliance
Lightning Source LLC
Chambersburg PA
CBHW020542220526
45463CB00006B/2167